MOTHER'S COMFORT

*A Devotional **for Baby's First Year***

MOTHER'S COMFORT

*A Devotional **for Baby's First Year***

MELISSA HEILAND

HENDRICKSON PUBLISHERS

A Mother's Comfort: A Devotional for Baby's First Year

© 2011 Hendrickson Publishers Marketing, LLC
P. O. Box 3473
Peabody, Massachusetts 01961-3473

ISBN 978-1-61970-493-0

For more information, please contact:

Melissa Heiland
mheiland@comcast.net
www.beautifulfeetinternational.com

Printed in the United States of America

First Hendrickson Edition Printing — July 2014

This book is dedicated to the courageous women who choose to give life to their children despite overwhelming odds. It has been my honor and privilege to meet you and pray with you. You are brave, strong, and selfless. May God continue to bless you.

Acknowledgments

Thanks first of all to my Lord and Savior Jesus Christ. All good things come from him.

Thanks to my husband, Ken, who always shows me God's love through his actions.

Thank you to my children: Michael, Josh, Melissa, Jack, Andy, and Nick. May God continue to guide and protect you each and every day.

Thank you to the many men and women who work tirelessly in pregnancy care centers because of their love for God and for women. I especially want to thank my co-laborers at Central Florida Pregnancy Central. Locking shields with you is a joy.

Dear friend...

Congratulations! You are embarking on the beautiful, precious journey of motherhood. Whether this is your first child or your sixth, this is an amazing, challenging time of your life. I hope and pray that, as hard as it is, you will set aside time with the Lord to do this devotional. I believe the Lord will encourage you as you take time in his word.

There is a place for you to reflect and record your thoughts as you work through this book. I hope it will serve as a special remembrance of these amazing days as you grow closer to your child and your Heavenly Father. I pray that God will bless both you and your child!

Love and blessings,
Melissa

A Baby's Protection

Read Exodus 2:1–10

Then his sister asked Pharaoh's daughter, "Shall I go and get one of the Hebrew women to nurse the baby for you?" (v. 7)

God's people, the Israelites, were living peacefully in Egypt when the Egyptian king began to fear them. He feared that because of their number they would rise up and fight against him, so he devised a plan whereby all baby Israelite boys would be put to death. Moses was born under this law, but Moses' mother chose to protect her son. She hid him for three months, and when she could hide him no longer she built a waterproof basket as a bassinette and placed him in the Nile River. She sent his sister to watch and wait to see how God would provide for her baby.

And provide he did! The king's own daughter heard the baby's cries, and her heart went out to him. When Moses' sister saw the princess with her brother, she asked her if she would like her to find a woman to nurse the infant. When the princess agreed, Miriam returned with their own mother, who served as a nursemaid to her son until he was old enough to be weaned. Then his mother took him to the palace, and the princess raised him as her own. What a beautiful story of a mother's determined love and care and God's provision! This mother stood against the odds and protected her baby from evil and destruction, and God placed the child in a palace as a prince!

Just as God made a way for Moses, he will provide for you and your baby. Even if circumstances look bleak, keep looking up. God loves you and your baby, and he will make a way.

Father, help me to be strong and resourceful like Moses' mother. Thank you that you will care for me and my baby and that we can trust in you. We love you. Amen.

Write your prayer for your baby.

A Gift from God

Read 1 Samuel 1

"I prayed for this child, and the LORD has granted me what I asked of him. So now I give him to the LORD." (vv. 27–28)

Hannah was infertile. Although her husband loved her with all his heart, she cried often and was brokenhearted. She begged God to give her a son. She promised him that if he would give her a son, she would give the child back to him. God answered her heartfelt cries and gave her a son, whom she named Samuel, which means "heard of God." And Hannah kept her promise. As soon as Samuel was weaned, she brought him to the temple to learn to serve God. Samuel grew up to be a mighty man of God.

Maybe, like Hannah, you waited many years for the birth of your child. Or maybe the birth of your baby was not at all expected or wanted. Either way, your child is a gift from God, and God has great plans for your baby's life. The Lord has given you this precious gift, and now you must make a choice to give your child back to God. Raise your child to love and serve God all of his life. Trust God to answer your prayers and his.

Father, thank you for giving me this beautiful baby. Help me to raise him to serve and obey you. Help me to give him back to you. Amen.

What are you trusting God for?

Mother's Womb

Read Psalm 139

For you created my inmost being;
you knit me together in my mother's womb.
I praise you because I am fearfully and wonderfully made;
your works are wonderful,
I know that full well. (vv. 13–14)

As you look into your baby's eyes, you see the work of God's hand. He knit your baby together in your womb. It is overwhelming to think that this child was formed and grew within your own body. Our God is amazing! And just as God knows everything about your baby, he knows everything about you. You are also his special creation.

As David, the writer of this psalm, reminds us, God knows our thoughts and our ways. In every situation and circumstance, God is there holding on to you, protecting you and your baby. His thoughts concerning you are more numerous than the grains of sand. You are his precious child. Rest in the knowledge that God made you wonderful.

Thank you, God, for my baby. You have made her wonderful. I thank you that you have made me wonderful too. Help me today to rest in you, to know that you are always with me. Help me to feel your presence. Amen.

Describe the baby God has given to you.

A Promise of Blessing

Read Proverbs 20:7

The righteous man leads a blameless life;
blessed are his children after him.

What a promise! God says that if we lead a righteous life, our children will be blessed by God. This is a tremendous promise, but you may wonder: How can I be righteous? Surely God sees my heart and my life, and he knows the wrong I have done.

Galatians 3:6 says, "*Consider Abraham: 'He believed God, and it was credited to him as righteousness.'*" God knows that you are not righteous on your own. His word says, "*All our righteous acts are like filthy rags*" (Isaiah 64:6). So how can we be righteous and gain blessing for our children? Through faith in Jesus. "*God made him who had no sin to be sin for us, so that in him we might become the righteousness of God*" (2 Corinthians 5:21). Believe God today, and you will be credited with righteousness. Jesus has paid the price so that you can be righteous, and God will bless your children.

Thank you, Father, that you have blessed my child. I thank you that Jesus paid the price for me so that I can be righteous before you. I know that I don't deserve this, but I am grateful for your love and blessings for me and my child. Amen.

Write a prayer of thanksgiving to God.

A Promise for the Future

Read Proverbs 22:6

*Start children off on the way they should go,
and even when they are old they will not turn from it.*

The Bible is full of promises. You may have been disillusioned in your life by people who broke their promises to you. Broken promises cause broken hearts and broken lives. But God cannot break his promises. He is always true and faithful. God promises us as mothers that if we train our children to do what is right, they will not turn away from what is right when they are old.

This is a great responsibility for us. How do we know what is right? We follow the Bible. We study God's word, and we pray. Of course there will be hard days and times of discouragement. But we can hold on to God's promise to us for our children. Our task is difficult, but it brings great rewards.

> Father, I thank you that you are a God who can be trusted. You always keep your promises. Help me to train my child in the way he should go. And I thank you that when he is old he will do what is right. Thank you, Father. Amen.

Tell God what you dream for your child.

A Promise of Rest

Read Matthew 11:28–30

*"Come to me, all you who are weary and burdened, and I will
give you rest. Take my yoke upon you and learn from me, for
I am gentle and humble in heart, and you will find rest for
your souls. For my yoke is easy and my burden is light."*

Caring for a baby can be very hard work. I remember
walking around like a zombie the first few weeks of each of my
children's lives. Jesus tells us that if we come to him, he will give
us rest. You may be carrying many burdens—financial strain,
troubled relationships, health issues. Jesus tells us to give our
problems to him.

Our troubles may be overwhelming, much more than we can
bear alone. The wonderful truth is that we are not alone. Jesus
is willing and able to carry our burden. The Bible says, *"Cast
your cares on the L*ORD *and he will sustain you; he will never let
the righteous be shaken"* (Psalm 55:22). Jesus can give you not
only rest for your body but also rest for your weary soul. Trust
him today.

Thank you, Father, that I can cast all of my cares on you. You
know every circumstance in my life, and I trust you to take
care of me. Thank you that I can find peace and rest in you.
Amen.

What are you trusting God for today?

A Mother's Comfort

Read Isaiah 66:13

"As a mother comforts her child,
so will I comfort you."

As a mother, one of your primary jobs is to comfort your baby. When she is wet, you change her. When she is hungry, you feed her. When she is lonely, you hold her. God will do the same for you, my sister. When the days are dark and cold, he will bring you warmth and light.

"*When Jesus spoke again to the people, he said, 'I am the light of the world. Whoever follows me will never walk in darkness, but will have the light of life'*" (John 8:12). When you are hungry for wisdom and discernment, he will feed you with his word. "*Then Jesus declared, 'I am the bread of life. Whoever comes to me will never go hungry, and whoever believes in me will never be thirsty'*" (John 6:35). And when you are lonely, he will comfort you. The Lord said, "*No one will be able to stand against you all the days of your life. As I was with Moses, so I will be with you; I will never leave you nor forsake you*" (Joshua 1:5).

> Heavenly Father, I am grateful that you comfort me as I comfort my baby. Help me to be a good mother. I pray in Jesus' name, amen.

Tell God what is troubling you.

Cords of Kindness

Read Hosea 11:1–4

I led them with cords of human kindness,
with ties of love.
To them I was like one who lifts
a little child to the cheek,
and I bent down to feed them. (v. 4)

The Israelites were God's children. They had been freed from slavery by God, but they turned their backs on him. They were living completely wayward lives, going so far as to sacrifice to idols. Yet their Heavenly Father had compassion on them. God reached out to them in loving-kindness, even in their sin. He lifted the chains of bondage from their necks and bent down from his heaven to tenderly feed them.

Perhaps today you are enslaved. You may be trapped in the bondage of sin—alcohol, drugs, ungodly relationships, lying, or vanity. You may be rebelling against God, taking control of your own life. Your Father longs to reach down from heaven and remove the chains that bind you. Turn to him, and he will lead you to a place of freedom and safety. There you will find rest as he gives all that you need from his tender and mighty hand.

Lord, thank you for kindness and love. Forgive me for my rebellion. I turn my back on the sins that enslave me and turn to you as my Savior and Lord. In Jesus' name, amen.

What would you like to be free from?

The Greatest in the Kingdom

Read Matthew 18:1–6

*"And whoever welcomes a little child like this
in my name welcomes me."* (v. 5)

Jesus loves children. Over and over again, we see this in his word. In fact, when the disciples asked Jesus "Who is the greatest in the kingdom of heaven?" he responded by calling over a little child and telling the disciples they had to change and become like little children in order to enter heaven. God wants us to be like little children—willing to trust and follow without fear.

And Jesus went on. He told us that when we welcome a child in his name, we welcome him. Jesus rejoices as you love your child.

And then he warned the disciples. He said that if anyone caused a child to sin, he'd be better off drowned in the sea!

Rejoice, my sister, in the knowledge that Jesus loves you and your baby. As you care for your baby, you are making Jesus smile. And be careful, dear sister, to teach your child to follow the Lord. You have been given a great responsibility. Handle her carefully.

Father, thank you for loving me and my baby. Help me to teach her to always follow you as I seek to do the same. In Jesus' precious name, amen.

Thank God for loving you and your baby.

Jesus' Blessing

Read Mark 10:13–16

*And he took the children in his arms, put his
hands on them and blessed them.* (v. 16)

Throngs of people were following Jesus. The Bible says they
were bringing little children for him to place his hands on them.
But the disciples were acting like bodyguards, sending the children away. Maybe they thought Jesus was too important to bother
spending time with children. Their actions made Jesus indignant.
The very idea that he wouldn't want to be with the children was
offensive to Jesus. You see, Jesus' heart is especially tender toward
children. He wants us to receive his kingdom like little children,
trusting completely.

Even now, Jesus reaches down from heaven, taking you and
your baby in his arms, blessing you both. You see the way your
baby looks to you to fulfill his needs. He finds everything he
needs in your arms—strength, tenderness, love, protection. You
can find the same safety in the arms of Jesus. Trust him with your
life today.

Thank you, Jesus, for your tender care. Help me to trust you
like my baby trusts me. I know you will take perfect care of
us. Amen.

Tell God how you love him.

Do Not Forget

Read Deuteronomy 4:9–14

*Only be careful, and watch yourselves closely so that you
do not forget the things your eyes have seen or let them
fade from your heart as long as you live.* (v. 9)

Think of the blessings God has given you in your life. It is easy for us to focus on what we do *not* have, but today think of your blessings. Look into the eyes of the child God has given you and be thankful for the life God has entrusted to you. Never let the fact that your child is a blessing slip from your heart.

Sometimes we get overwhelmed with bills and busyness and the worries of life. Today is the day we remember God's blessings. Are there people in your life who have cared for you, listened to you, encouraged you? Do you have a roof over your head and food for yourself and your child? Do you have your own copy of God's word, the Bible? Do you have a Savior who has reached down to you and saved you?

Father, I am so thankful for all you have done for me. I thank you for the privilege of being able to talk to you as your daughter. I thank you for my beautiful baby. I pray in Jesus' name, amen.

List your blessings.

What Do These Stones Mean?

Read Joshua 4:4–7

"In the future, when your children ask you, 'What do these stones mean?' tell them that the flow of the Jordan was cut off before the ark of the covenant of the LORD." (vv. 6–7)

In order to enter the land that God had promised the Israelites, they had to cross the Jordan River. The priests were to carry the ark of the covenant, which contained the very presence of God. When God's people arrived at the river's edge, the Jordan was at flood stage. But as soon as their feet touched the water's edge, the water from upstream piled up in a heap at a town far away, and the water flowing down to the sea was completely cut off. The priests stood firm on dry ground in the middle of the river, while the whole nation crossed on dry ground (Joshua 3:15–17). God instructed them to put down stones as a memorial as to how God provided for them.

Think about what God has done for you. Make a memorial so you can tell your child about how God has blessed you. Put down stones or plant a tree.

Lord, I thank you for the gifts you have given me. Help me to remember to tell my child about your provision. Amen.

Write a letter to your child about how God has taken care of you.

How Majestic Is Your Name

Read Psalm 8

LORD, our Lord,
how majestic is your name in all the earth!
You have set your glory
in the heavens.
Through the praise of children and infants
you have established a stronghold against your enemies,
to silence the foe and the avenger. (vv. 1–2)

The same God who placed the moon and stars in the sky is concerned about you. He cares about your job, your school, your bills, and your baby. If it matters to you, it matters to God. Tonight, pause to look into the heavens. See the glory of God's handiwork, and know that God is looking down on you just as you lovingly look at your child. Praise his name. Sing to the Lord of his majesty and glory.

As you hold your baby, sing to her about the love of Jesus. Sing a song that you learned as a child. Sing Psalm 8 or make up your own song of praise. Your baby will smile as you sing, and so will Jesus.

Lord, our Lord, how majestic is your name in all the earth!

Write a song of praise to Jesus.

Have No Fear

Read Psalm 112

Surely the righteous will never be shaken;
they will be remembered forever.
They will have no fear of bad news;
their hearts are steadfast,
trusting in the LORD. (vv. 6–7)

This psalm describes the lives of those who trust and obey God. They are blessed, and their children are strong. Good comes to them, as they are generous with others. Even in tough times, they see the light at the end of the tunnel. They give to the poor. They are not afraid, because they trust in the Lord. If you love and obey Jesus, you are one of those.

There may be times when fear niggles at our mind. Say aloud, "I have no fear of bad news. My heart trusts in the Lord." God will give you a peace that passes understanding. He will guard your heart and your mind in Jesus (Philippians 4:7). You and your children are blessed. It's a promise from God. Even when the world around you is crumbling, you can count on Jesus.

Thank you, Lord, that I am blessed and that my children will be mighty. Help me not to be afraid but to trust in you. Amen.

Write out portions of Psalm 112 and claim these promises as your own.

True Beauty

Read Proverbs 31

Charm is deceptive, and beauty is fleeting;
but a woman who fears the LORD is to be praised. (v. 30)

It's hard to be a woman in our society. We are constantly bombarded with messages about being beautiful and young and thin and perfect. We feel we can never measure up to the models we see on television and in magazines. It can be very difficult to see these unrealistic images day after day. The message we receive is that our value is in our looks. Our looks determine who and what we are. This is a lie.

God's word is truth. It tells us that charm and beauty are deceptive and fleeting. True beauty is found in the woman who respects and honors the Lord. If you follow the Lord in your life, your children will call you blessed. Your child and your God both see the beautiful woman you are because of your love for Jesus. Be the beautiful godly woman you were created to be.

God, I thank you that you created me and made me beautiful. Help me to focus on inner beauty, which comes from obedience to you. Help me to remember that I am special because you love me. Amen.

List the characteristics that make you beautiful (for example, loving, patient, generous, and so on).

Our Defender

Read Isaiah 49:25

*"I will contend with those who contend with you,
and your children I will save."*

Sometimes we face opposition in our lives. It may be a jealous co-worker or an angry neighbor. Sometimes it is even a family member who is behaving like an enemy. Jesus makes it clear that he is our defender. Don't worry, my sister. If you are following Jesus, he's got your back.

Continue to do the right thing even when others around you are cheating and lying and hurting others to get ahead. Tell the truth. Treat people with respect and kindness. Trust God to fight your battles for you. He says that he will contend with those who contend with you. He will save your children.

Our culture tells us to look out for number one. The message of the Bible is different. God's word tells us to love our enemies and turn the other cheek. God is on your side if you are obeying him. And if God is for us, who can be against us? (Romans 8:31).

Thank you, God, for being my shield and defender. Help me to do the right thing, even when others around me are not. I trust you. Amen.

In what area in your life do you need to trust God?

Do Not Worry

Read Matthew 6:25–34

"But seek first his kingdom and his righteousness, and all these things will be given to you as well." (v. 33)

It seems like motherhood and worrying go hand in hand. We worry about what our children eat, what they wear, when they sleep, and if they are developing on schedule. Then we worry about where they will go to school and who they will marry. We can keep ourselves up all night long worrying about our babies.

But God has a different plan. He tells us that we have no need to worry, because he will lovingly care for us and our babies. He tells us to look at how he feeds the birds and cares for the lilies. And he reminds us that we are much more valuable to him than they are. God tells us that we need to follow him and he will give us everything we need. The best way for us to care for our children is to study God's words and God's ways and put them into practice in our lives. Follow him each day, and trust him to take care of your child.

> Father, I thank you that you have promised to take care of me and my child. Help me to learn your ways and to obey. In Jesus' name, amen.

Make a list of things you are trusting God to handle.

Receiving Gifts

Read Matthew 7:7–11

"For everyone who asks receives; the one who seeks finds; and to the one who knocks, the door will be opened." (v. 8)

You love your child so much! When you look into her little face, you want to give her the world. You want to protect her from all harm and make her dreams come true. That is also how God feels about you!

If you have accepted Jesus as your Savior, you are God's daughter. And as hard as it is to imagine, God loves you even more than you love your baby! He longs to protect you and give you gifts. He wants you to ask him to provide for you. Sometimes we feel that we don't want to bother God with our needs and our desires. But his word tells us that he will give gifts to those who ask. Do you have a need or dream for yourself or your child? Tell God. He is eagerly waiting to bless you with answered prayer!

Lord, I thank you that you are a loving, kind, and generous Father. You know my needs, my hopes and my dreams for me and my child. Please give me the desires of my heart as I follow you. Amen.

Write a prayer asking God to make your dreams come true.

You Are Valued

Read Matthew 10:29–31

"And even the very hairs of your head are all numbered." (v. 30)

Sometimes we feel invisible, as if no one even sees us or cares that we exist. We feel completely alone. Nothing could be further from the truth. Do you realize that God knows how many hairs are on your head? He cares about you so intimately that he knows each and every detail about you. He knows when you brush your hair and when a tear falls from your eye. The Bible tells us that God keeps our tears in a bottle (Psalm 56:8).

When you cry alone in the darkness of night, God is there with you. You are never really alone, because God is always by your side, caring about the things that are in your heart and mind. Speak to him through prayer. Let him calm your fears. Listen to his voice by reading your Bible. He will remind you, "Don't be afraid. You are worth so much to me." God loves you enough to send his son to die for you. You have great value to God.

Father, thank you for loving me and caring about all the things I care about. I trust you to take care of me. Amen.

Write your own prayer thanking God for valuing you so highly.

Compassionate Giving

Read Mark 6:30–37

When Jesus landed and saw a large crowd, he had compassion
on them, because they were like sheep without a shepherd.
So he began teaching them many things. (v. 34)

Jesus and his disciples had been serving people all day long. The Bible tells us that because so many people were coming and going, they decided to take a boat and get away from the crowds for a while and rest. However, as they were leaving, people recognized them, and people from all the towns ran ahead and waited for them. When Jesus landed and saw the large crowd, even though he was exhausted he had compassion on the people. Although he had planned to rest for a while, because of his great love for the people he taught them many things instead of resting. His disciples advised Jesus to send the people away to buy food, but Jesus responded by telling the disciples to give them something to eat. The result is a miracle of feeding five thousand!

Because you are a mother, you are very often exhausted. You want time to rest, but it seems your baby always needs you. Jesus knows how it feels to keep going when your body needs rest. Look to him as your example, and trust him to give you strength.

Thank you, God, for your loving example of selfless giving. Help me to follow your example as I give to my child. Amen.

Write a description of what you and your baby have done today.

Praying Together

Read Matthew 18:19–20

"For where two or three gather in my name, there am I with them." (v. 20)

God did not intend for us to live our lives alone. He knows that we need other people who will help us and strengthen us and encourage us. Sometimes we become isolated as mothers. It seems like the whole world is contained in the circle of us and our child. This can leave us feeling alone. God tells us to pray with other believers. He tells us that when we pray with one or two other people, he is there with us. His word says that when two people on earth agree about something and ask God for it, it will be done (Matthew 18:19).

There is power in numbers. Think today about someone who will agree with you and pray with you. Maybe you don't know anyone in your area, but you can call or text a friend or family member who will pray with you. Look for a local church or mothers' group where you can find people who will support you.

God, I pray that you will help me to find a godly friend who will pray with me. Thank you for answering prayers. Amen.

Make a list of people who will pray with you.

Doing the Impossible

Read Luke 1:26–38

"For nothing is impossible with God." (v. 37, NLT)

When you look at your baby, you see a miracle. Your baby is a miracle. But imagine how Mary, Jesus' mother, felt as she looked at her child. Her child was conceived and grew in her womb even though she was a virgin. Her child was the Son of God!

Your child may have been planned or he may have been conceived in very difficult circumstances. Regardless of the circumstances surrounding his conception, your child is a gift. No matter how challenging your life is, nothing is impossible with God. If a virgin could give birth to a child, anything is possible. God specializes in the impossible.

Just as God saw Mary, a poor young girl living in a tiny town, God sees you and has a special plan for your life and for the life of your child. You may be facing circumstances that seem utterly hopeless—financial crisis, health crisis, broken relationships, and broken dreams. Remember Luke 1:37 and believe it in your heart.

God, I know that nothing is impossible for you. I am asking you to make a way where there seems to be no way. In Jesus' name, amen.

What impossible things are you asking God to accomplish in your life?

Sit at the Lord's Feet

Read Luke 10:38–42

"Martha, Martha," the Lord answered, "you are worried and upset about many things, but few things are needed—or indeed only one. Mary has chosen whatr is better, and it will not be taken away from her." (vv. 41–42)

Mary and Martha were sisters. Jesus was visiting them. Mary sat at Jesus' feet listening to him while Martha was distracted by all the preparations that had to be made. She was busy cleaning, cooking, and decorating. Frustrated, she finally asked Jesus if he could see that she was doing the work all by herself. *"Tell her to help me!"* she cried.

Martha did not get the answer she was hoping for from Jesus. Jesus told her that Mary had made the better choice. Jesus was saying that it's better to take time with him, listening to his word, than to be busy with all the work. This is a hard lesson to learn. When the laundry is piling up and the dishes are in the sink, sitting down to read the Bible and pray is not easy to do. What would people think? But the question really is, what does God think? And we have his answer here in the Scriptures.

Father, help me to choose what is better. Help me take time each day to sit at your feet and listen. Amen.

Are you like Mary or Martha?

Guard against Greed

Read Luke 12:13–21

Then he said to them, "Watch out! Be on your guard against all kinds of greed; life does not consist in an abundance of possessions." (v. 15)

There are lots of discussions revolving around working mothers versus stay-at-home mothers. Some women have to work, some choose to work, and some choose to stay home. Every situation is different, and we should be careful not to judge each other. However, we do need to be careful. Clearly, our first priority is our children. The reason some women work is for their children, to feed and clothe them and to set an example of hard work.

We must examine our motives. God's word warns us to be on our guard against greed. It is important to be able to separate needs from wants. Our children are young for a short time. We want to spend as much time with them as possible, nurturing them. We will never regret time spent with our children.

Father, help me to evaluate my life and my choices. Guide me to make decisions that honor you. In Jesus' name, amen.

Evaluate your situation. Do you work or stay home? Are you making the best choice? Why or why not?

The Way to Heaven

Read John 14:1–7

*Jesus answered, "I am the way and the truth and the life.
No one comes to the Father except through me." (v. 6)*

Jesus tells us not to let our hearts be troubled, because he has prepared a place for us. That place is heaven. God's word tells us that heaven is a place where there is no sorrow, sickness, death, or tears. Heaven is a beautiful place, and our hearts long to go there one day. Jesus tells us that he is the only way to get to heaven.

No one is capable of getting to heaven by herself. We are not perfect and never will be. Our sin separates us from God. But God loves us so much, he sent Jesus to die in our place, to take the punishment for our sins. Jesus died on the cross and rose again. Eternal life with God in heaven is a gift. We cannot earn it; we must accept it. If you have never accepted this free gift of salvation, you can do it now. Admit that you are a sinner and that you need God. Believe that Jesus died on the cross for you and that he rose again. Confess Jesus as your Lord and Savior.

> Dear God, I know that I am a sinner and need forgiveness. I believe that Jesus died for me and that he rose again. I want to follow Jesus with my life. Thank you for saving me. In Jesus' name, amen.

Write a prayer thanking God for sending Jesus to die for you so you can live with him in heaven.

A Purpose for Me

Read Acts 17:24–31

"From one man he made all the nations, that they should inhabit the whole earth; and he marked out their appointed times in history and the boundaries of their lands." (v. 26)

God has a plan for us! This verse tells us that God has a very specific plan for us that includes the exact places where we should live. You may not be living in your dream house, but God has a plan for you where you are. Never think that the circumstances in your life are random or accidental. God has a purpose for you where you are.

The previous verse tells us that God is not far from each one of us. *"He himself gives everyone life and breath and everything else"* (Acts 17:25). Look around today. Are there people who need a word of encouragement? Is there someone who needs your help? As you push your baby in his stroller, pray for the people who pass by. Ask God to show you his purpose for placing you where you are.

> God, I want to serve you here and now. Help me to look for ways to help people you have put in my life. In Jesus' name, amen.

Make a list of people in your life and ways you can help them.

Good Deeds

Read 1 Timothy 5:9–10

She is . . . well known for her good deeds, such as bringing up children, showing hospitality, washing the feet of the saints, helping those in trouble and devoting herself to all kinds of good deeds.

All day long you are changing diapers, rocking your baby, and cleaning up all kinds of messes. It seems like a never-ending cycle. The days are long, and the nights are longer. Mothering can be a thankless job, much less glamorous than many other jobs.

Notice that when God is listing good deeds, he lists "bringing up children" first. You are doing a good deed as you care for your child each day. It may seem as if no one notices, but God notices, and he commends your good work. Be encouraged as you are caring for your baby. He will grow up so fast, giving you time for other things—showing hospitality and helping those in trouble. In the meantime, treasure your moments with your baby. Whisper words of love in his ear. Those words will go with him all of his life.

Father, thank you for my baby. Help me to be a good mother. Amen.

Write about your baby. What makes your child special?

Godly Mothers

Read Titus 2:3–5

*The older women . . . can urge the younger women to love
their husbands and children, to be self-controlled and pure,
to be busy at home, to be kind, and to be subject to their
husbands, so that no one will malign the word of God.*

This passage talks about older women teaching younger women. Do you have a godly woman in your life who can teach you? Don't feel like you have to figure everything out for yourself. Mothering is difficult! There are so many decisions to make.

The Bible tells us that young women need to be trained to love their husbands and train their children. You may be blessed with a mother or grandmother who can help you to be a godly mother. If not, pray for God to send someone to teach you to be self-controlled, pure, busy at home, and kind. I believe with all my heart that he will answer your prayers. A Bible-teaching church is a good place to find such a woman. MOPS (Mothers Of Preschoolers) is a great organization to join for this purpose. Observe godly mothers and learn from their example. Ask them to teach you. They will be honored, and you and your child will be blessed.

Father, please send someone into my life who can teach me to love my child. Thank you for hearing and answering prayers. In Jesus' name, amen.

Make a list of women you can ask to teach you to love your child. If you don't know a godly mother, list places you can go where you are likely to find one.

Trusting God

Read Genesis 50:15–21

"You intended to harm me, but God intended it for good to accomplish what is now being done, the saving of many lives." (v. 20)

Joseph was his father's favorite child. As a result, his brothers hated him. In fact, they hated him so much that they decided to kill him. They threw him in an empty well to die and then sat around to eat a meal. When they looked up, they saw a group of men coming and decided to sell their young brother as a slave rather than kill him. They then went home and told their father that Joseph had been devoured by a ferocious animal.

As it turned out, Joseph was bought by a very powerful man, who trusted Joseph with all he had. Ultimately, Joseph was put in charge of the whole land of Egypt. His brothers ended up going to Egypt to buy food because of a famine in their land. Guess who they had to buy food from? The brother they sold into slavery! When they realized who he was, they were terrified. But Joseph forgave them. Joseph's own brothers were unthinkably cruel to him, yet God used this circumstance to bless Joseph richly. Though sold as a slave, he was put in charge of all of Egypt.

Has someone close to you betrayed you? Are you in a terrible situation? Trust God to work it out for you.

Father, thank you for caring for me even though others mistreat me. I trust you to bring good out of every circumstance in my life. I love you. Amen.

What circumstance are you trusting God with now?

The Gentle Shepherd

Read Psalm 23 and Isaiah 40

He tends his flock like a shepherd:
He gathers the lambs in his arms
and carries them close to his heart;
he gently leads those that have young. (Isaiah 40:11)

Sheep without a shepherd are vulnerable. They eat food that makes them sick. When they fall, they are unable to get up. Wolves devour them. When the shepherd is with them, he leads them to green pastures and quiet waters. They don't need to fear wild animals, because the shepherd protects them. If they fall, he gently lifts them up.

Jesus is our shepherd. With Jesus, we have nothing to fear. He is our protector, our provider, and our comforter. He gathers us in his arms and carries us close to his heart. We can relax in his arms, knowing that he is holding us close.

As you comfort and protect your child, Jesus is caring for you. The Bible tells us that Jesus gently leads those that have young. His heart is especially tender toward you. Goodness and mercy will follow you all the days of your life if you trust in Jesus.

Jesus, thank you for your tender, loving care. Amen.

Write a prayer thanking God for the ways he has cared for you.

God's Hands

Read Isaiah 49:15–16

"Can a mother forget the baby at her breast
and have no compassion on the child she has borne?
Though she may forget,
I will not forget you!
See, I have engraved you on the palms of my hands;
your walls are ever before me."

This passage begins with a rhetorical question: "*Can a mother forget the baby at her breast and have no compassion on the child she has borne?*" Of course not! A mother loves her child all the days of her life. She has no choice. Yet the Lord says, "*Though she may forget, I will not forget you!*"

He is making a point. As much as you love your child, God loves you more. Never think that you are not on God's mind. He has engraved you on the palms of his hands. Picture God's hands with your name engraved on them. You are always on his mind. You are the apple of God's eye (Psalm 17:8). Christ's hands have scars from the piercings of the nails when he went to the cross so that you could live with him forever in heaven. You are that important to God.

Father, we praise your mighty name. We cannot understand the depths of your love for us, but we thank you for it. Thank you for your constant love and care. In Jesus' name, amen.

Draw a picture of God's hands with your name on them.

The Teacher

Read Isaiah 50:4–5

*He wakens me morning by morning, wakens my ear
to listen like one being instructed.* (v. 4)

The Lord has much to teach you! Whether you have known the Lord since childhood or have just begun your relationship with him, there is so much to learn. God is always seeking to teach us—through nature, circumstances, other people, prayer, and especially the Bible.

Each morning as you awaken, it is the Lord who wakens you (perhaps by the means of a crying baby!). He wakens your ear to listen to what he wants to teach you. He wants to teach of his love for you and of his tender mercies that are new each day. He wants to teach you how to love and forgive others the way he has forgiven you. He wants to teach you to be kind and compassionate and obedient. He wants to teach you how to be a good mother. Are you listening?

Father, thank you for awakening me each day. Help me to listen and learn all that you want me to know. Amen.

Take a moment and listen to God. What is he teaching you?

A New Heart

Read Ezekiel 36:25–30

"I will give you a new heart and put a new spirit in you; I will remove from you your heart of stone and give you a heart of flesh." (v. 26)

Have you ever felt hard-hearted, like your heart was made of stone? I have. Sin can cause our hearts to harden. At times, like the Israelites, we choose to worship idols. We probably don't literally bow before statues, but we do value money, power, prestige, beauty, and popularity more than we value Jesus. We prioritize worldly things over heavenly pursuits, and our hearts become stony. Or someone hurts us deeply and rather than forgive, we harden our hearts as a defense. We think if our hearts are hard we are safe; no one will be able to hurt us again.

But when our hearts are hard, we cannot fully give and receive love. We cannot enjoy the life of love that God has planned for us. God gives us the solution: ask him for a new heart. He will give us a new heart and a new spirit, one that is free to worship him.

Father, remove my heart of stone. Give me a new heart, a clean heart that can fully worship you and love others. Thank you for your wonderful works. Amen.

What are the idols in your life? What things come between you and God? Confess them now.

Depths of the Sea

Read Micah 7:18–19

You will again have compassion on us;
you will tread our sins underfoot
and hurl all our iniquities into the depths of the sea. (v. 19)

We all sin against God. We all make choices that are selfish and wrong, and these choices separate us from God. But *"if we confess our sins, he is faithful and just and will forgive us our sins and purify us from all unrighteousness"* (1 John 1:9). God tells us in his word that he does not stay angry forever but delights to show mercy. God tells us that he will again have compassion on us.

You may have made a mess of your life. Perhaps you have made one bad decision after another. It is never too late to repent, to turn your life around. God does not tire of forgiving us. When we confess our sins, he forgives us. In fact, he throws our sins into the depths of the sea.

Sometimes other people will unkindly remind us of our past failures. Many times we replay our bad choices over and over again in our minds, but God never does. Christ died for our sins. He has removed our sins from us as far as the east is from the west (Psalm 103:12).

Today is the day to turn your life around. If you have a lifestyle of sin, confess it to God, accept his forgiveness, and start fresh. God will be delighted, and so will you.

Father, I confess my sins to you. Thank you that because of Jesus, my sins will not be held against me. I pray in Jesus' precious name, amen.

What sins will you turn from?

Quieted with His Love

Read Zephaniah 3:17–20

"The LORD your God is with you,
the Mighty Warrior who saves.
He will take great delight in you;
in his love he will no longer rebuke you,
but will rejoice over you with singing." (v. 17)

You hold your baby in your arms and are prepared to protect him from anyone or anything that might ever hurt him. He is safe in your arms. You are likewise safe in the arms of Jesus. He is mighty to save you from anything or anyone who would harm you.

You take great delight in your child. It brings you great joy to hold your child and watch him smile. That is how Jesus feels about you. He takes great delight in you. When your baby cries, often all he needs is to be held by you. As you hold him and rock him, he quickly quiets down because he feels your love for him. So it is with Jesus. When you begin to worry and fret, Jesus will quiet you with his love.

As you sing to your baby, listen to Jesus rejoicing over you with his singing. Allow Jesus to hold you and quiet you. Meditate on how great his love and care for you are. Rest in the strong, tender arms of your Savior.

Thank you, Jesus, for the peace and quiet I feel as I rest in your love. Amen.

Draw or write a description of the peace you have in Jesus.

A Mother's Sacrifice

Read 1 Kings 3:16–27

The woman whose son was alive was deeply moved out of love for her son and said to the king, "Please, my lord, give her the living baby! Don't kill him!" (v. 26)

The Bible tells us a story of two women who came to the king to settle a serious dispute. They had both recently given birth, and one of their babies had died. The first woman claimed that the other woman's baby had died and she had taken her baby from her side while she slept and placed the dead child at her breast. The second women vehemently denied this. She insisted that the living child was hers. To settle the dispute, the king asked for a sword and ordered that the living child be cut in two, giving half to each woman. One woman agreed that this was fair, and the other woman begged for the child's life to be spared. She pleaded with the king not to harm the child but to give him to the other woman. The king wisely gave the child to the woman who had begged for the child's life to be spared, realizing that she was truly the child's mother.

This is the essence of motherhood, sacrificing your own desires for what is best for the child. Although it broke her heart to let the child go, the mother would have gladly suffered to spare her child pain. As your child grows, you will make many sacrifices for his benefit. This is the calling of motherhood.

Thank you, God, for the gift of my child. Help me to follow you as I parent my child. Amen.

What did God sacrifice for you? Write him a prayer of thankfulness.

The Wise Woman

Read Proverbs 14:1

The wise woman builds her house,
but with her own hands the foolish one tears hers down.

None of us wants to be foolish; we all wish to be wise. The Bible offers us simple words of wisdom—build your house; don't tear it down. This does not refer to laying drywall and pouring concrete. Building your house means building up and encouraging the people in your house. Who lives in your house—parents, husband, friend, children? Build them up.

Living together, building a home with others, is always difficult. Personalities, lifestyles, and tastes will clash. Make it your goal to be a peacemaker. The Bible says, *"Blessed are the peacemakers, for they will be called children of God"* (Matthew 5:9). When conflict arises, be the one who is calm and kind. Even though someone else has wronged you, respond with kindness. God's word says, *"Be kind and compassionate to one another, forgiving each other, just as in Christ God forgave you"* (Ephesians 4:32). As you encourage those around you, you will be a blessing to them and God will bless you.

Father God, it is hardest to be kind at home. Please help me to forgive others as you have forgiven me. Help me to use my words to build up, not to tear down. I love you. Amen.

How will you build up the people in your house?

Honor Your Parents

Read Exodus 20:1–12

*"Honor your father and your mother, so that you may live
long in the land the LORD your God is giving you." (v. 12)*

Everyone has heard of the Ten Commandments, the rules
for living that God gave to his people through his servant Moses.
Some of these commands seem much harder to keep than others.
Today I want to focus on the fifth commandment—honor your
father and your mother. This commandment is not only for children, but for adults as well.

The Lord has commanded us to honor our parents. The Bible
does not say to honor our parents if they are honorable; it tells
us to honor our parents, period. As adults, we are not required
to obey our parents, but it is our duty to honor them. This means
we must speak to them respectfully. We must talk about them
respectfully. We must never be rude or condescending to them.
The Lord requires this of us, and he gives us a promise: if we
honor our parents, we will live long lives. We want our children
to honor us when we are old. We must set an example for them as
we strive to honor our parents with our words and actions.

Father, help me to honor my parents. I need your help to
forgive them and to treat them with respect. I pray that my
children will honor me as well. I pray in Jesus' name, amen.

How will you show honor to your parents?

A Mother's Legacy

Read 2 Timothy 1:3–5

*I have been reminded of your sincere faith, which first
lived in your grandmother Lois and in your mother Eunice
and, I am persuaded, now lives in you also. (v. 5)*

Timothy was a man of God. He was a faithful servant. The
Bible tells us that his grandmother, Lois, was a woman of faith.
As a godly mother, she raised her daughter, who also became a
woman of faith. In turn, Eunice lived a life of faith, and her son,
Timothy, became a man of faith.

Never underestimate your influence as a mother. You will
make mistakes along the way; we all do. But if you live a life of
faith, a life of looking to God for direction and trusting him to
supply your needs, your children will notice. They watch you to
see if you turn to God in good times and in bad. You can give
your children a great gift, a legacy of sincere faith. You may not
have great riches to leave to your child, but a legacy of faith is
more valuable and lasting than vast sums of wealth.

Father, help me to have faith in you. Help me to teach my
child with my words and with my actions that I have faith in
you. Thank you for your faithfulness. In Christ's name, amen.

How can you leave a legacy of faith for your child?

From My Mother's Womb

Read Psalm 22:9–10

From birth I was cast upon you;
from my mother's womb you have been my God. (v. 10)

I don't know when you began to trust God. Maybe you have followed him all of your life or maybe you are just beginning your journey with God. Regardless, your desire is for your baby to follow Jesus all of her life. God's word tells us that a life of following God can begin very young. Your child does not have to wait until she has made great mistakes and suffered from the consequences of wrong choices. She can follow God all the days of her life.

The Bible speaks of trusting in God at your mother's breast. What comfort this gives to you! Your baby can have the care and protection of God from the beginning. As you teach her to walk and to talk and to feed herself, you can also teach her to pray and to sing praises and to trust God in all things. You can help her to develop habits of going to church and reading the Bible and turning to God in all situations.

Father, I thank you that you have been my baby's God even from the womb. Thank you that she is trusting you even at my breast. You are a great and loving God! Amen.

Write a description of your baby.

Your Reward

Read Psalm 127

*Children are a heritage from the LORD,
offspring a reward from him.* (v. 3)

Your child is a reward from God, a blessing for you. You may be facing very difficult circumstances in your life, but God has given you a great blessing amid the trials. Your baby is your reward. In this psalm, the Lord reminds us that "*unless the LORD builds the house, its builders labor in vain*" (Psalm 127:1). Build your life on the solid rock of Jesus. As you make decisions about work, money, housing, and childcare, seek God's will. Pray. Read your Bible. Follow God's plan. He will guide you in all of your decisions. He will protect you and your baby.

This psalm reminds us that everything we do is a waste of time if we are not following God. Then God tells us, "*He grants sleep to those he loves*" (Psalm 127:2). What a beautiful promise for new mothers! Your baby may be getting you up and keeping you up at all hours of the night, but God loves you and will give you sleep. And because God is protecting you and your baby, you can sleep peacefully, knowing you are in good hands.

Thank you, Father, for your love and care. Thank you for my child. Help me to raise him to love you. Amen.

Write about how your baby has blessed you.

God's Plan for You

Read Jeremiah 29:11–14

"For I know the plans I have for you," declares the LORD, "plans to prosper you and not to harm you, plans to give you hope and a future." (v. 11)

God has a plan for you. You can trust him. Sometimes we are tempted to take control of our lives. You may have people in your life who were supposed to take care of you but didn't. Maybe your parents hurt you or failed to protect you from others. Maybe your baby's father abandoned you. So you are tempted to harden your heart and take control of your life. That will only bring you more heartache.

God is the perfect Father. He promises never to leave you (Joshua 1:5). People will disappoint you. God never will. God has a plan for you, and his plan is to prosper you and to give you hope. God's plans are always for your best. He loves you and will always protect you.

Don't try to take control of your own life. God can be trusted to always do what is best for you. He will listen to you. He will be found by you. If you have been taken captive by sin or sorrow, he will rescue you and bring you back to the safety of his arms. Run into his arms today.

> Lord, I don't want to take control of my life. I surrender my life to you. I believe that your way is always best. I will follow you where you lead. In Jesus' precious name, amen.

Write your own prayer to God, giving him control of your life.

Love

Read 1 Corinthians 13

And now these three remain: faith, hope and love.
But the greatest of these is love. (v. 13)

With the birth of your child, you are learning about love in a whole new way. You may have experienced love in the past, but the love a mother has for her child is a new and wondrous thing. You may not be sure exactly how to love your child. God has devoted this chapter to describing love to us.

He tells us that love is patient. Mothering requires lots of patience. Love is kind. It is not easily angered. You may have a temper, but as you learn to love your child, you will learn to control that. Love always protects. Because you love your baby, you protect her. Love always hopes. You may face situations now or in the future that seem hopeless, but because of love, you will have hope in spite of the circumstances. Love always perseveres. There may be times that you feel like giving up, but you will not, because of love. Love never fails. God loves you with unfailing love. Because of his love and care for you, you can love and care for your child.

Lord, thank you for loving me and for teaching me to love my child. Fill my heart and life with you. Amen.

Write a love letter to your child.

God's Power

Read Ephesians 3:14–21

*Now to him who is able to do immeasurably more than all we
ask or imagine, according to his power that is at work within
us, to him be glory in the church and in Christ Jesus throughout
all generations, for ever and ever! Amen.* (vv. 20–21)

God has great things in store for you! God has glorious
riches, and out of his riches, he strengthens you with power
through his Spirit, who lives and works in you. If you have re-
ceived Jesus as your Savior, you have the Holy Spirit within you.

Are you feeling weak? Be strengthened by God's power.
Christ's love for you is wide and long and deep and high. God
is able to do so much more than we could ever ask or imagine.
And his power is at work within you. Imagine that—God's power
working within you! You need never feel weak or helpless or de-
feated. God is on your side. If God is for you, who can be against
you (Romans 8:31)?

When you receive Christ as Savior, the Holy Spirit comes into
your heart and life and empowers you to live a life of love, a life of
purpose. Don't be afraid. Dream big. God's plans for you are even
more glorious than you can imagine!

God, I thank you for saving me through Jesus Christ. I thank
you for your love and your power. Help me to know your
love and be strong in you. In Jesus' name, amen.

What do you dream of doing for God?

Everything Is Possible

Read Mark 9:14–29

"Everything is possible for one who believes." (v. 23)

The Bible tells the story of a man whose son was possessed by a spirit, which had rendered him mute. It would cause him to have seizures, throwing him to the ground, rigid and gnashing his teeth. The boy's father told Jesus that the spirit had often thrown his son into water or fire to kill him. The father had asked the disciples to drive out the spirit, but they were unable to do it. In desperation, the father brought the boy to Jesus. He asked Jesus to help them if he could.

Jesus was astonished that the father questioned whether Jesus was able to help them. Jesus told them that everything is possible for the one who believes.

You may have worries about your child. Maybe he is sick or handicapped. Like this father, bring your child to Jesus. The boy's father told Jesus, *"I do believe; help me overcome my unbelief!"* (Mark 9:24). God will erase your doubts as you come to him in faith. Nothing is impossible for God. Trust him today.

> Father, I want to trust you completely. Help me overcome my unbelief. I believe that everything is possible through you! I love you. Amen.

What impossible thing can God do for you?

WEEK 46

Forgiven

Read Luke 7:36–50

"Therefore, I tell you, her many sins have been forgiven—as her great love has shown. But whoever has been forgiven little loves little." (Luke 7:47)

Do you ever feel ashamed of your past, afraid to approach God because of your past sins? In this passage of the Bible, Jesus was having dinner with religious leaders when a woman who had lived a publicly sinful life came to Jesus, crying, kissing his feet and pouring perfume on them. The religious leaders criticized Jesus for allowing this sinful woman to touch him.

Jesus responded to this by telling a story. He told a story of two men who owed money; one owed ten times more than the other. Both of their debts were forgiven—they did not have to repay the money they owed. Jesus asked, who would love the money lender more, the man whose small debt was forgiven or the man whose large debt was forgiven? The answer, of course, was the man with the larger debt. Because the money lender had not required him to repay a large sum of money, he was tremendously grateful.

You may be like this woman in the story who was guilty of many sins. If you have confessed your sins to God and believed in Christ to forgive you, you are completely forgiven. Jesus welcomes you into his presence. Your many sins are forgiven. Worship freely at Jesus' feet.

Father, I confess to you that I am a sinner. Thank you for saving me. I praise your holy name. Amen.

Confess your sins. Praise the Lord.

Lacking No Good Thing

Read Psalm 34

The lions may grow weak and hungry,
but those who seek the LORD lack no good thing. (v. 10)

Taste and see that the Lord is good (Psalm 34:8)! Never doubt God's goodness. God is wholly and completely good. Everything he does is good, without exception.

Those who seek the Lord lack no good thing. This is a prevailing theme in the Bible. Trials will come in your life. You will experience sorrow, but with God, sorrow is never the end of the story. "*Weeping may stay for the night, but rejoicing comes in the morning*" (Psalm 30:5). God is our healer, our deliverer, our refuge. He gives us all good things because he loves us. Today is the day to praise him and thank him for who he is and what he has done for us.

If you feel you are lacking something in your life, seek the Lord. God's word tells us he is close to the brokenhearted. A righteous woman may have many troubles, but the Lord delivers her from them all (Psalm 34:19). If you are in need, cry out to the Lord. His ears are attentive to your cry. He loves you and will provide for you in everything.

Father, I thank you for your great provision for me. I thank you that you hear my cries and that I lack no good thing because I seek you. In Jesus' name, amen.

Tell the Lord what you need. Thank him for providing for you.

Choose Life

Read Deuteronomy 30:11–20

This day I call the heavens and the earth as witnesses against you that I have set before you life and death, blessings and curses. Now choose life, so that you and your children may live and that you may love the Lord *your God, listen to his voice, and hold fast to him.* (vv. 19–20)

We are faced with choices every day. Some are trivial (mustard or mayonnaise?), and others have great importance. Some choices are life-altering. When you discovered you were pregnant, you had a choice. Maybe it was an agonizing decision. The fact that you are reading this book means you chose life. What a beautiful decision that you will never regret! You gave your child the most precious gift—the gift of life. No one else could do that.

The Lord is pleased with your decision. He knows what it cost you, and he will bless you greatly through this child. As you continue to love the Lord and obey him, he will continue to bless you. Continue to look to God and walk in his ways. Following God will not always be easy, but it will always bring peace and joy and blessings for you and for your child.

> Father, thank you for the gift of life. I thank you for my life and for the life of my child. Help me to follow you all of my days. In Jesus' precious name, amen.

Write about your baby.

Great Responsibility

Read Deuteronomy 6:1–9

*Impress them on your children. Talk about them when
you sit at home and when you walk along the road,
when you lie down and when you get up. (v. 7)*

The Lord has done great things for you! Think back over your
life and remember the times that God protected you. Think of the
people he has put in your life to help and encourage you. Remember the people who taught you about Jesus' love. God has had his
hand on you from your mother's womb.

God tells us to love him with all our hearts, minds, souls, and
strength (Mark 12:20). He tells us not only to keep his commands
on our hearts but also to teach them to our children. This is
not something to be done every once in a while, but daily. God
tells us to teach our children about him when we sit, when we
walk, when we lie down, and when we get up. He tells us to tie
his commands over our hands or bind them on our foreheads
(Deuteronomy 6:8).

We are to be teaching our children about God at all times.
This is a great privilege and responsibility. It is good to bring your
child to Sunday school and church and Vacation Bible School, but
it is not enough. Your child needs to hear God's word from *your*
mouth. Tell your child about who God is and how he loves her.
Begin today.

Father, You are great and mighty. No one compares to you.
I pray that my child will follow you all of her life. Amen.

Write a letter to your child about God's goodness.

Living by Faith

Read Romans 8:28–39

And we know that in all things God works for the good of those who love him, who have been called according to his purpose. (v. 28)

Life here on earth can be difficult. This is true for God's people as well. God's people suffer loss along with those who reject God. Christians get sick, lose jobs, get divorced, and lose loved ones. We live in this world of sin, and we are not exempt from suffering.

The difference for those of us who follow Christ is that God works all things for the good of those who love him. None of us wants to suffer, yet we trust our God to work good through the suffering. Suffering causes us to draw closer to God as we trust him despite what we see. That is faith, being certain of what we do not see (Hebrews 11:1). We can be sure that God always has our best interests at heart. And so we live by faith and not by sight (2 Corinthians 5:7), knowing that absolutely nothing will be able to separate us from the love of God in Christ our Lord (Romans 8:38–39).

> Father, I thank you that you are working all things for good in my life. I thank you that you have called me according to your purpose. I praise your name. Amen.

Give an example from your life of something God has worked out for your good.

Spiritual Milk

Read 1 Peter 2:1–3

*Like newborn babies, crave pure spiritual milk, so that
by it you may grow up in your salvation, now that you
have tasted that the Lord is good.* (vv. 2–3)

Watch your baby as she eagerly sucks at the breast or bottle. She is eager for the milk. This is how God wants us to approach his word, hungrily. When we receive Christ as Savior, the Bible says we are born again. As newborns we need milk to grow, spiritual milk. This milk is God's word. It nourishes our spirit as milk nourishes a baby's body.

Without milk, a baby will not grow properly. If we do not spend time reading and studying the Bible, our spirits will not grow properly. Your baby will only go so long without milk before she cries for it. We should be the same. We should hunger for God's word and not be satisfied by anything else.

Babies need to eat every day. So do we. Open your Bible each day to be fed in your spirit now that you have tasted that the Lord is good.

Father, feed me with your word. Teach me what I need to know. Show me what you want me to do. Amen.

What has God taught you in his word?

Broken Chains

Read Psalm 78:1–8

So the next generation would know them,
even the children yet to be born,
and they in turn would tell their children. (v. 6)

Sometimes families experience generational sin. This is when a sin is committed by a parent or parents and then repeated by children and grandchildren, generation after generation. A father abuses his child, who in turn abuses her child, who abuses her child. A daughter of an alcoholic becomes an alcoholic herself, whose son abuses alcohol as well.

It doesn't have to be this way. Even if there is generational sin in your family, a new pattern can be established through God, beginning with you! You do not have to be like your forefathers. Through Christ, you are a new creation. The chains of sin no longer hold you captive. You are free to worship God and serve God and be the godly woman God designed you to be. Confess your sin to God, and he will empower you to create new patterns for your children, grandchildren, and generations to come.

Father, I thank you that you have broken the chains of sin. Sin has no power over me, because of Jesus Christ's completed work on the cross. Thank you that new patterns of godly living begin with me. In Jesus' precious name, amen.

What sinful patterns will you break through Christ's power?
Write a prayer of your own, thanking God for broken chains
and victorious living.